FRACTIONS AND DECIMALS
Workbook Math Essentials
Children's Fraction Books

All Rights reserved. No part of this book may be reproduced or used in any way or form or by any means whether electronic or mechanical, this means that you cannot record or photocopy any material ideas or tips that are provided in this book

Copyright 2016

Fun math activities help improve children's understanding of fractions and decimals.

Missing Numbers

Fill in the missing numbers.

1. $\dfrac{\boxed{}}{20} = \dfrac{1}{4}$

2. $\dfrac{16}{\boxed{}} = \dfrac{8}{10}$

3. $\dfrac{\boxed{}}{32} = \dfrac{5}{8}$

4. $\dfrac{\Box}{18} = \dfrac{3}{9}$

5. $\dfrac{2}{3} = \dfrac{\Box}{9}$

6. $\dfrac{3}{4} = \dfrac{20}{\Box}$

7. $\dfrac{4}{\boxed{}} = \dfrac{12}{27}$

8. $\dfrac{3}{\boxed{}} = \dfrac{1}{5}$

9. $\dfrac{12}{16} = \dfrac{3}{\boxed{}}$

10. $\dfrac{\square}{30} = \dfrac{4}{6}$

11. $\dfrac{30}{36} = \dfrac{5}{\square}$

12. $\dfrac{6}{8} = \dfrac{\square}{40}$

13. $\dfrac{8}{16} = \dfrac{\square}{8}$

14. $\dfrac{3}{4} = \dfrac{\square}{8}$

15. $\dfrac{5}{6} = \dfrac{10}{\square}$

16. $\dfrac{5}{\boxed{}} = \dfrac{30}{36}$

17. $\dfrac{1}{10} = \dfrac{2}{\boxed{}}$

18. $\dfrac{\boxed{}}{7} = \dfrac{15}{21}$

19. $\dfrac{2}{\Box} = \dfrac{6}{21}$

20. $\dfrac{1}{3} = \dfrac{6}{\Box}$

21. $\dfrac{\Box}{20} = \dfrac{2}{4}$

22. $\dfrac{1}{5} = \dfrac{4}{\boxed{}}$

23. $\dfrac{\boxed{}}{3} = \dfrac{4}{6}$

24. $\dfrac{6}{60} = \dfrac{1}{\boxed{}}$

25. $\dfrac{21}{\Box} = \dfrac{7}{9}$

26. $\dfrac{\Box}{10} = \dfrac{18}{30}$

27. $\dfrac{\Box}{15} = \dfrac{3}{5}$

28. $\dfrac{25}{35} = \dfrac{\Box}{7}$

29. $\dfrac{\Box}{40} = \dfrac{6}{8}$

30. $\dfrac{1}{10} = \dfrac{\Box}{50}$

31. $\dfrac{18}{30} = \dfrac{3}{\Box}$

32. $\dfrac{12}{24} = \dfrac{\Box}{4}$

33. $\dfrac{\Box}{5} = \dfrac{18}{30}$

34. $\dfrac{1}{4} = \dfrac{\square}{20}$

35. $\dfrac{5}{7} = \dfrac{30}{\square}$

36. $\dfrac{2}{5} = \dfrac{6}{\square}$

37. $\dfrac{2}{10} = \dfrac{1}{\boxed{}}$

38. $\dfrac{2}{\boxed{}} = \dfrac{10}{50}$

39. $\dfrac{1}{\boxed{}} = \dfrac{4}{36}$

Add and Subtract Decimals

9923.77
- 1752.45

....

8641.39
- 5574.52

$$3730.69 \\ +3585.19 \\ \overline{}$$

....

$$8634.82 \\ +9855.56 \\ \overline{}$$

$$9637.41$$
$$+4304.88$$
―――――――

$$8462.15$$
$$+8480.85$$
―――――――

$$6752.65 \\ +\,8448.75 \\ \overline{}$$

$$7084.31 \\ -\,5317.33 \\ \overline{}$$

$$4475.64$$
$$+2647.42$$
$$\overline{}$$

....

$$6045.37$$
$$+3968.94$$
$$\overline{}$$

```
  7980.57
- 3355.57
_____
```

· ·

```
  8211.83
- 1955.61
_____
```

$$9801.98 - 8684.73$$

$$4157.72 + 9319.49$$

$$8480.27 + 6975.79$$

....

$$6752.42 - 2616.96$$

$$9711.37 + 3878.86$$

. . . .

$$2941.18 - 1104.95$$

$$5007.91 + 5049.67$$

⋯⋯⋯⋯⋯⋯⋯⋯⋯⋯⋯⋯⋯⋯⋯⋯⋯⋯⋯⋯⋯⋯⋯

$$5909.73 - 5356.96$$

```
  219.16
+ 441.38
---------
```

```
  677.33
+ 901.48
---------
```

```
  408.83
+ 296.77
_____
```

```
  347.26
- 297.72
_____
```

```
  167.18
+ 839.43
---------
```

....

```
  739.73
- 145.24
---------
```

$$709.21$$
$$-\ 153.91$$

· ·

$$617.23$$
$$-\ 177.25$$

$$971.37$$
$$+902.75$$
───────

$$659.93$$
$$-\ 339.34$$

$$469.66$$
$$+712.46$$
_____

$$204.29$$
$$-177.52$$
_____

ANSWERS

1. $\dfrac{5}{20} = \dfrac{1}{4}$

2. $\dfrac{16}{20} = \dfrac{8}{10}$

3. $\dfrac{20}{32} = \dfrac{5}{8}$

4. $\dfrac{6}{18} = \dfrac{3}{9}$

5. $\dfrac{2}{3} = \dfrac{6}{9}$

6. $\dfrac{3}{4} = \dfrac{15}{20}$

7. $\dfrac{4}{9} = \dfrac{12}{27}$

8. $\dfrac{3}{15} = \dfrac{1}{5}$

9. $\dfrac{12}{16} = \dfrac{3}{4}$

10. $\dfrac{20}{30} = \dfrac{4}{6}$

11. $\dfrac{30}{36} = \dfrac{5}{6}$

12. $\dfrac{6}{8} = \dfrac{30}{40}$

13. $\dfrac{8}{16} = \dfrac{4}{8}$

14. $\dfrac{3}{4} = \dfrac{6}{8}$

15. $\dfrac{5}{6} = \dfrac{10}{12}$

16. $\dfrac{5}{6} = \dfrac{30}{36}$

17. $\dfrac{1}{10} = \dfrac{2}{20}$

18. $\dfrac{5}{7} = \dfrac{15}{21}$

19. $\dfrac{2}{7} = \dfrac{6}{21}$

20. $\dfrac{1}{3} = \dfrac{6}{18}$

31. $\dfrac{10}{20} = \dfrac{2}{4}$

32. $\dfrac{1}{5} = \dfrac{4}{20}$

33. $\dfrac{2}{3} = \dfrac{4}{6}$

34. $\dfrac{6}{60} = \dfrac{1}{10}$

35. $\dfrac{21}{27} = \dfrac{7}{9}$

36. $\dfrac{6}{10} = \dfrac{18}{30}$

37. $\dfrac{9}{15} = \dfrac{3}{5}$

38. $\dfrac{25}{35} = \dfrac{5}{7}$

39. $\dfrac{30}{40} = \dfrac{6}{8}$

40. $\dfrac{1}{10} = \dfrac{5}{50}$

41. $\dfrac{18}{30} = \dfrac{3}{5}$

42. $\dfrac{12}{24} = \dfrac{2}{4}$

43. $\dfrac{3}{5} = \dfrac{18}{30}$

44. $\dfrac{1}{4} = \dfrac{5}{20}$

45. $\dfrac{5}{7} = \dfrac{30}{42}$

46. $\dfrac{2}{5} = \dfrac{6}{15}$

47. $\dfrac{2}{10} = \dfrac{1}{5}$

48. $\dfrac{2}{10} = \dfrac{10}{50}$

49. $\dfrac{1}{9} = \dfrac{4}{36}$

9923.77	9637.41	4475.64	9801.98	9711.37
− 1752.45	+ 4304.88	+ 2647.42	− 8684.73	+ 3878.86
8171.32	13942.29	7123.06	1117.25	13590.23

8641.39	8462.15	6045.37	4157.72	2941.18
− 5574.52	+ 8480.85	+ 3968.94	+ 9319.49	− 1104.95
3066.87	16943.00	10014.31	13477.21	1836.23

3730.69	6752.65	7980.57	8480.27	5007.91
+ 3585.19	+ 8448.75	− 3355.57	+ 6975.79	+ 5049.67
7315.88	15201.40	4625.00	15456.06	10057.58

8634.82	7084.31	8211.83	6752.42	5909.73
+ 9855.56	− 5317.33	− 1955.61	− 2616.96	− 5356.96
18490.38	1766.98	6256.22	4135.46	552.77

219.16	347.26	709.21	659.93
+ 441.38	− 297.72	− 153.91	− 339.34
660.54	49.54	555.30	320.59

677.33	167.18	617.23	469.66
+ 901.48	+ 839.43	− 177.25	+ 712.46
1578.81	1006.61	439.98	1182.12

408.83	739.73	971.37	204.29
+ 296.77	− 145.24	+ 902.75	− 177.52
705.60	594.49	1874.12	26.77

www.ingramcontent.com/pod-product-compliance
Lightning Source LLC
LaVergne TN
LVHW061322060426
835507LV00019B/2266